tiny treats

By Julia A. Monroe

★ American Girl™

Questions or comments? Call 1-800-845-0005,
visit our Web site at **americangirl.com**, or write to
Customer Service, American Girl, 8400 Fairway Place, Middleton, WI 53562-0497.

Printed in China

06 07 08 09 10 11 LEO 10 9 8 7 6 5 4 3

All American Girl marks are trademarks of American Girl, LLC.

Editorial Development: Trula Magruder

Art Direction: Camela Decaire

Production: Kendra Schluter, Mindy Rappe, Jeannette Bailey, Judith Lary

Photography: Radlund Photography

Stylists: Tricia Doherty, Jim Rude, Jackie Shanahan

Cataloging-in-Publication Data available from the Library of Congress.

A special thanks to our testers:
Allie K., Clove H., Katie D., Kelsey H., Lauren C., Libby T.,
Maddie P., Natalie H., Rosie L., and Shelby H.

dear reader,

These tiny treats make super snacks for bitty

birthdays, small sleepovers, pixie

picnics, and tiny tea parties. From the button-sized

pie and sweet cinnamon rolls to the peewee

wedding cake and cute croissants—

these treats taste as great as they look!

Your friends at American Girl

table of contents

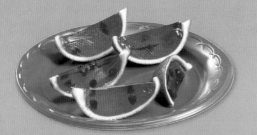

getting started

Check out these important tips before you start.

- When you see this hand ![hand icon], ask an adult to help you, especially if you're working with a sharp knife, the oven, or the microwave.

- Read over the recipe and gather your ingredients and supplies before starting.

- Always wash your hands before and during cooking. Friends and family won't want to eat marshmallows with your fingerprints all over them.

- Sometimes it's easier to cut food with kitchen scissors. Ask first, and be sure the scissors are clean.

- Work on wax paper. It makes sticky fruit leather, sprinkles, and other messy foods easier to work with and keeps treats cleaner.

frosting tips

Frost like a baker by following these tips!

- Use *whipped frosting* to decorate cakes. It's soft and easy to spread. Use *icing* to stick foods together. Icing is sticky and makes a good food "glue."

- Cold frostings are hard to use, so let them warm to room temperature.

- For convenience, look for pre-bagged frostings in your grocery store.

- When you use a frosting (or pastry) bag, fill the bag with ¼ cup of frosting, then attach a chip clip across the bottom of the bag so the icing won't squeeze out.

- If you use a pastry bag with tips, don't worry if the frosting looks crooked. You'll get better with practice. Try "piping" an edge around a plate rim or writing on wax paper.

chef secrets

There's more than one way to have fun with your cute creations!

serve them up

Invent unique ways to serve mini treats
to friends and family. For a pixie picnic,
spread a bandanna over a picnic basket,
then add fun mini accents. Try a small
flower pot or a tiny bucket of crushed
ice filled with candy wax bottles.

show them off

Display your treats for all to see. For
instance, stack tiny candy perfume
bottles in a bead organizer.

give them away

To make treats even sweeter, share them with someone special. Does your teacher like tea? Slip petit fours into a teacup with pretty teabags and cute sugar cubes, then tie on a ribbon.

play with them

Think of ways to spotlight your playful foods. Put a candy ladybug on a paper leaf or tuck a tasty bonnet into a papier-mâché hatbox.

bitty breakfast

Always start your day with a little breakfast!

eggs and sausage

A doll's dish makes a
great breakfast plate!

- adult's help
- 2 white candy melts
- 2 yellow M&M's
- Tootsie Roll Midgee
- cheese grater
- 2 French Toast
  Crunch cereals
- candy orange slice

Serve up a Sunday feast!
With an adult's help,
microwave melts for
1 minute. Press an M&M
into each melt. Shape
Tootsie Roll pieces into
link sausages, then lightly
roll them on the grater.
Arrange treats on a plate
with the cereal and
orange candy.

waffles

Whip up a batch of bitty
waffles on a winter day.
Cut waffle-shaped cookies
into squares with a butter
knife. Add your favorite
toppings.

12

doughnuts and milk

Take home a variety of doughnuts hot off the line! Use Multi-Grain Cheerios for plain doughnuts or toss some in a sandwich bag with powdered sugar.

★ With an adult's help, melt 2 tablespoons of chocolate chips. Dip the cereal tops in chocolate, adding sprinkles to some. (If a hole gets clogged, poke it clean with a toothpick.) Let set. Serve with milk.

Arrange the doughnuts in a tiny box lined with tissue paper.

13

croissants

Curl up with a cute croissant!

- ⭐ adult's help
- single crescent roll triangle, unbaked
- rolling pin
- pizza cutter
- baking sheet

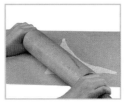

1. Ask an adult to help with this recipe. Preheat oven to 375 degrees. Unroll dough and flatten with rolling pin until thin as a tortilla.

2. Cut dough into small triangles. Make wide end of each triangle about 2 inches. Start at wide end, and roll triangle to tip.

3. Pinch down tip. Curl croissant ends into crescent. Lay on baking sheet. Bake croissants for 8 minutes. Let cool on sheet.

For chocolate croissants, ask an adult to melt a few chocolate chips in a microwave. Drip chocolate on with a toothpick.

cinnamon rolls

These sweet rolls look like they came from a bed and breakfast inn!

YOU WILL NEED

- ⭐ adult's help
- rolling pin
- unbaked home-style refrigerated biscuit
- flour
- baking sheet
- ½ teaspoon butter
- ½ teaspoon cinnamon
- 1 teaspoon sugar
- small bowls
- kitchen scissors
- 1 ½ teaspoons water
- 2 tablespoons powdered sugar

1. Ask an adult to help with this recipe. Preheat oven to 375 degrees. On floured baking sheet, roll out biscuit until thin as a pancake. Spread butter on top.

2. Mix cinnamon and sugar in bowl, sprinkle mixture onto biscuit, then roll biscuit lengthwise into snake. Pinch edges. Cut dough into tiny slices.

3. Bake rolls for about 8 minutes. Let cool slightly. Mix water and powdered sugar in bowl until smooth. Dip tops of warm rolls in glaze.

petite picnic

Pack up a picnic with lots of finger foods.

sub sandwiches

Hide these small subs or your picnic could turn into a block party!

With an adult's help, slice the pepperoni, onion, and tomato. Cut the cheese into smaller squares. Slice the bread stick in half lengthwise and then into 2-inch pieces. Tear off tiny pieces of lettuce. Layer toppings on the bread. Hold sandwiches together with fancy toothpicks.

YELLOW MUSTARD

8 OZ. (226g)

watermelon

The best thing about this watermelon is that you can eat the seeds!

With an adult's help, cut both limes in half. Clean out the fruit with a spoon. Make half a box of Jell-O, following the Jiggler directions on the box. Lay the lime rinds in the tin and spoon in Jell-O. Chill until nearly firm. Use the skewer to push chocolate chips into the Jell-O. Chill again until firm, then cut into slices.

Use green sprinkles to make "parsley!"

deviled eggs

The sweetest eggs you'll ever eat!

- ⭐ adult's help
- ¼ cup sugar
- ½ teaspoon water
- small bowl
- almonds
- ¼ cup white candy melts
- spoon
- yellow mini M&M's
- fork

1. Mix sugar and water in bowl. Smooth surface, press almonds into sugar to make imprints, then remove nuts.

2. With an adult's help, heat candy melts following package directions. Spoon candy into imprints. Top each with mini M&M.

3. Refrigerate until eggs harden, then lift them out of sugar with fork. Brush off loose sugar. To make more eggs, smooth sugar again.

s'mores

Try this campfire favorite! Lay a **mini marshmallow** on a **Golden Graham cereal square** and a **chocolate chip** on another cereal square. Put the pieces on a microwaveable plate.  With **an adult's help,** heat the s'more in a **microwave** for 8 to 10 seconds. Squish the pieces together!

small state fair

Surprise friends with small fair snacks!

caramel popcorn

A large popcorn, please! With an adult's help, melt 2 teaspoons butterscotch chips in the microwave. With a spoon, stir in 2 teaspoons each of crunchy peanut butter and powdered sugar. Add ½ cup puffed wheat cereal, then blend it into the mixture with your hands. Spread the cereal on wax paper, and place in the fridge until firm.

Decorate a small disposable cup and fill it with popcorn.

pepperoni pizza

YOU WILL NEED

- adult's help
- paring knife
- snack-size pepperoni stick
- refrigerated French loaf, unbaked
- baking sheet
- pizza sauce
- grated cheese

Serve this pizza as an appetizer. With an adult's help, heat the oven to 375 degrees and cut the pepperoni into thin slices. Cut a ½-inch slice of dough from the loaf, then pat it out on the baking sheet. Spread on sauce and top with cheese and pepperoni. Bake until cheese melts.

strawberry shake

YOU WILL NEED

- fork
- 1 teaspoon pink lemonade powder
- 1 tablespoon strawberry yogurt
- ¼ cup whipped cream
- small bowl
- spoon and tiny glass
- pink sugar
- mini straw

This sweet shake will satisfy any thirst for flavor! Use a fork to mix lemonade powder, yogurt, and whipped cream together in a bowl. Spoon the shake into a tiny glass. Sprinkle sugar on top and tuck in the straw.

Use the cap from canned whipped cream for a really cool glass!

blue-ribbon pie

Take the top prize at the state fair with this personal-sized pie!

For each pie:
-  adult's help
- paring knife
- ice cream cone
- blueberry pie filling or jam
- ¼ cup almond paste
- toothpick
- sugar

1. With an adult's help, cut bottom off ice cream cone. Turn cone as you cut it. (Tip: crumble leftover tops over ice cream!)

2. Spoon blueberry pie filling or jam into cone bottom.

3. Roll almond paste into ball. Flatten ball with fingers, making a circle to fit over pie. Pinch edges with tooth- pick or fingers. Sprinkle with sugar.

Use a toothpick to cut out a fun shape on top!

26

ice cream cone

One dip or two? Use a **melon baller** to scoop out chilled **fruit-flavored or plain cream cheese**, and serve it in a **Bugles corn snack**.

wee bakery

Celebrate with cute cakes and petite pastries!

peanut butter kiss cookies

These cute cookies taste as good as their larger cousins. ✋ With an adult's help, preheat the oven to 375 degrees. Using your hands, roll marble-sized pieces of refrigerator peanut butter cookie dough in sugar, and lay them on a baking sheet. Bake cookies for 6 to 7 minutes, then top each one with a chocolate chip after they come out of the oven. Let cool.

jelly roll

This makes a great after-school snack! Remove crusts from a slice of bread, then flatten the bread with your hands. Spread jelly over the slice, then roll it into a snake shape. Cut into small pieces with a butter knife. Dust with powdered sugar.

petit fours

-  adult's help
- butter knife
- sugar wafer cookies
- 1/3 cup + 1 teaspoon powdered sugar
- 1/2 teaspoon corn syrup
- bowl
- 2 teaspoons hot water
- wax paper
- sprinkles

Add a little luxury to your tea parties with these fancy cakes. Cut the cookies into squares. Set aside. For a glaze, put the sugar and syrup in a bowl. Ask an adult to add hot water, and mix well. Slip the cookies into the glaze, then turn them over. Use a knife to move each cookie to the wax paper. Create small flowers with sprinkles.

31

birthday cake

- 5-inch cardboard circle
- aluminum foil
- 1 round ice cream sandwich
- butter knife
- whipped frosting
- frosting bag/star tip
- sprinkles
- thin cake candles

This petite party cake is the perfect cooler on a hot day. Cover the cardboard with foil, then place the ice cream sandwich on top. Frost the sandwich, then pipe a border around the top and bottom of the cake. Decorate with sprinkles. Trim the candles, then add them to the cake.

Keep the cake in the freezer until you're ready to serve it.

32

graduation sheet cake

YOU WILL NEED

- aluminum foil
- 4-by-5-inch piece of cardboard
- whipped frosting
- 2 toaster pastries
- butter knife
- frosting bag/star tip/writing tip
- candy flowers

Personalize a four-layer sheet cake for any occasion! Cover the cardboard with foil. Dab frosting on the foil, then place a toaster pastry on it. Frost the top of the pastry, lay the second pastry on top, then frost the top and sides. Fill the frosting bag. Put the star tip on the bag. Pipe an icing border around the top and bottom edges. Change to a writing tip (or use icing tubes made for writing) to create a message. Decorate with candy flowers.

special day cakes

Show a loved one you care with these dainty cakes.

For a plain cake:
- whipped frosting
- butter knife
- 2 sandwich cookies

1. Frost cookie. Lay second cookie on top. Frost top and outside of stack.

2. Decorate cake to suit special day, if desired.

3. Let cake soften overnight, then slice and serve.

Happy Valentine's! Frost vanilla sandwich cookies. Press coconut into frosting with fingers. Add heart sprinkles around border.

Mother's Day or Father's Day

Frost vanilla sandwich cookies. Decorate with sprinkles and spell out "Mom" or "Dad." Pipe on a border.

Company's coming!

Frost chocolate sandwich cookies. Crush a walnut with the back of a spoon. Sprinkle nuts around the edge.

wedding cake

Bridal guests will gush over a custom wedding cake.

YOU WILL NEED

- wax paper
- 3 vanilla sandwich cookies
- whipped frosting
- icing knife
- saucer, turned upside down
- frosting bag/star tip
- sprinkles
- 2 toothpicks, broken in half
- drinking straw cut into four 1-inch pieces
- 1-inch cookie cutter

1. On wax paper, frost top of one cookie. Lay second cookie on top, then frost top and sides of stack. Slip knife under cake and move it to saucer. Pipe on top and bottom borders. Add sprinkles.

2. Stick pointed ends of 4 toothpick pieces into cake center, keeping toothpicks at equal heights, then slip a straw piece over each one. Dab frosting on tops of straws, as shown.

3. To make cake top, cut third cookie with cookie cutter. Place on wax paper, frost, then pipe on a border. Add sprinkles. Let chill.

4. Slip knife under chilled cake top and gently place it on pillars. Re-pipe border, if needed.

sweet accessories

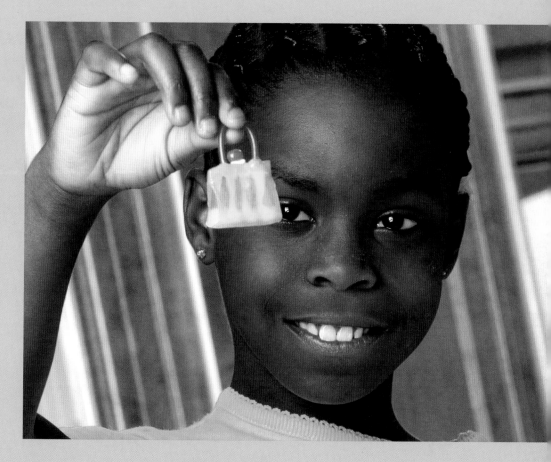

Show off your great fashion taste!

coin purse

YOU WILL NEED

- 3-by-1½-inch piece of wax paper
- Fruit Roll-Up sheet
- scissors
- tube icing
- candy corn
- licorice string
- red candy button

Use this "corn" purse for small shopping trips. Stick the wax paper to the Fruit Roll-Up sheet and cut around it. Remove the wax paper. Fold in each end of the cutout ¼ inch. Add the icing and candy corn, as shown. Slip in the licorice. Fold up the sides. Add a snap with icing.

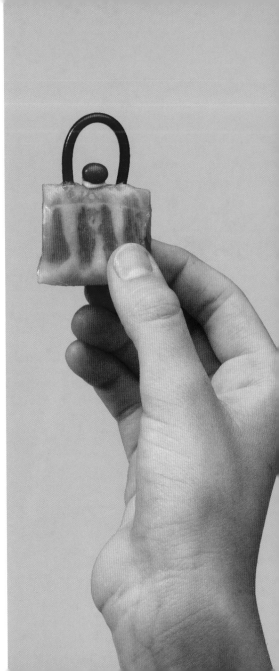

spring bonnets

These bitty bonnets will bring a splash of color to your table. With an adult's help, carefully cut the bottom off an ice cream cone with a paring knife. Stick the cone bottom to a vanilla wafer cookie with icing. Decorate with icing, sprinkles, Fruit Roll-Up sheets, and candies.

perfumes

Your friends will love this sweet gift! Dab icing on different candies with a toothpick to create perfume bottles.

flip-flops

Go ahead and put these shoes on the table! Lay a sheet of Fruit Roll-Up on wax paper. Place the cookies on the Roll-Up, and cut around them with a toothpick. Spread icing on the cookie top, then lay the fruit cutout over it. Press the sheet edges down to smooth them. For straps, stick candy straws on with icing. Decorate.

42

cowgirl hats

Yee-haa! Round up your partners for a taste of the West. With an adult's help melt dipping chocolate, following the package instructions. Slip a mini marshmallow on a toothpick, dip it in the chocolate, and set it on the top of a Swoops candy. Place on wax paper. Decorate. Cool in the fridge until firm.

bunny slippers

These small slippers make a great bedtime snack!

1. Working on wax paper, flatten large marshmallow with hands, then cut it in half.

2. Dip cut sides of marshmallows in colored sugar to prevent stickiness.

3. Press your finger into marshmallow to make inside of slipper. (Dip finger in sugar if it's sticky.)

4. Spread frosting across toe and around sides of slipper, then dip it in white nonpareils to cover frosting.

5. Attach nonpareil eyes and nose with frosting. Cut mini marshmallow in half. Press cut side in sugar, then attach ears with frosting.

Make a mix of slippers! For a pig, cut a mini marshmallow in half for a pig snout. For plain slippers, dip the front half in colored sugars.

little garden

Look in the garden for sweet inspiration!

butterflies

Make stomachs flutter with bitty butterflies!

1. With adult's help, melt candy, following package directions. Spread melted candy along walnut center with toothpick. Sprinkle on black sugar.

2. For wings, cover sides of walnut with more melted candy. Decorate with sugar and sprinkles.

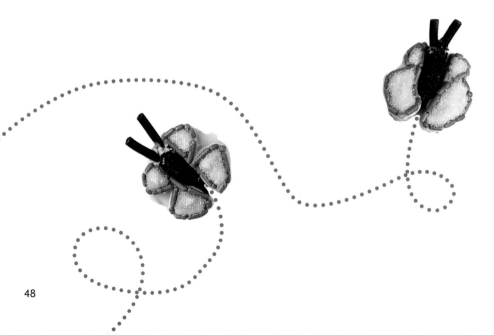

3. Dip tiny pieces of thin licorice in melted candy and stick onto butterfly for antennae.

dragonflies

These bugs will quickly fly into mouths! Use **scissors** to cut **Fruit Roll-Ups** into *very* small rectangles. Crisscross and stick them to **candy-coated licorice pieces** to look like wings. Use a **toothpick** to dot on **chocolate icing** for eyes.

ladybugs

It's easy to catch these little ladies! 🖐️ With **an adult's help**, melt a few **chocolate chips** in the **microwave**. Dip a **toothpick** into the chocolate to decorate an **M&M** like a ladybug. To make a straight line, let the chocolate drip into a thin string, then run it across the candy.

49

field of flowers

Create the prettiest indoor garden you've ever seen! For each flower, squeeze **white tube icing** onto a **Necco candy wafer**. Spread icing with a **butter knife**, then arrange **candies, sprinkles,** and **colored sugar**. Let dry.

51

flower pots

Pick your sweetest flowers and place them in a peewee pot!

- adult's help
- paring knife
- ice cream cone
- mini marshmallows
- toothpick
- pretzel sticks snapped in half
- gumdrops
- 1 tablespoon chocolate chips
- kitchen scissors
- sugar
- green icing
- 4 flowers (see page 50)

1. With adult's help, carefully cut top edge off ice cream cone, keeping bottom for pot. Stuff marshmallows into bottom of cone with toothpick.

2. Stick pretzel half in bottom of gumdrop. With adult's help, melt chocolate chips in microwave. Spread chocolate over marshmallows, then slip in pretzel. Repeat. Let cool in fridge.

3. For leaves, cut gumdrops into slivers, covering sticky sides with sugar. Spread icing between pretzel sticks. Press leaves into icing.

4. Spread icing on top of gumdrops. Press on flowers.

Now get creative
in the kitchen!
Gather your friends and
invent your own tiny treats.

And if you'd like, share your ideas with us. Send them to:

tiny treats editor
american girl
8400 fairway place
middleton, wi 53562

(Photos can't be returned. All comments and suggestions
received by Pleasant Company Publications may be used
without compensation or acknowledgment.)

Here are some other American Girl books you might like:

❑ I read it.

❑ I read it.

❑ I read it.

❑ I read it.

❑ I read it.

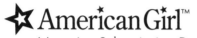

American Girl celebrates a girl's inner star—that little whisper inside
that encourages her to stand tall, reach high, and dream big. We take
pride and care in helping girls become their very best today, so they'll
grow up to be the women who make a difference tomorrow.

Questions or comments? Call 1-800-845-0005, visit our
Web site at americangirl.com, or write to Customer Service,
American Girl, 8400 Fairway Place, Middleton, WI 53562-0497.

8+   59792 $9.95
Printed in China

ISBN 1-58485-979-2

50995

9 781584 859796